GREAT LOVERS

paintings by Walter Dorin

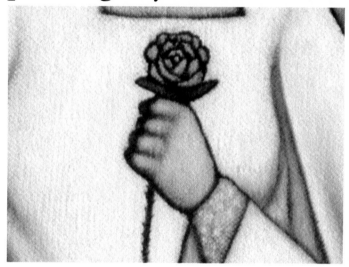

text by George Melly

JONATHAN CAPE
THIRTY BEDFORD SQUARE, LONDON

First published 1981
Text copyright © 1981 by George Melly
Illustrations copyright © 1981 by Walter Dorin
Jonathan Cape Ltd, 30 Bedford Square, London WC1

Walter Dorin's original works of art
are exhibited exclusively by Portal
Gallery Ltd, London, England.

British Library Cataloguing in Publication Data

Melly, George
Great Lovers
1.Love
I. Title   II. Dorin, Walter
306.7   GT2600

ISBN 0-224-01942-2

Printed in Italy by New Interlitho, Sp A, Milan

Contents

Introduction

The ancient theory is that each of us is incomplete, split by the malevolent gods from our other half for whom we must roam the world so that, in each other's arms, we can become our whole selves again; the two-headed, eight-limbed creature we once were.

'Have you any children?' the last Pope but two asked Louis Armstrong. 'No Pops,' Satchmo is alleged to have responded, 'but we've had a lot of fun trying.' So with our quest for completion. The difficulty is that seldom if ever do we meet the right demi-being. Perhaps most of us, when mutually attracted, imagine that this time we've found our alter-ego, but familiarity eventually proves our hopes a delusion. We may jog along, side by side in companionable affection until the edge of the grave, or turn away, in uncomprehending indifference or dislike, after a longer or shorter span, but total fusion, two forever one, is a great rarity.

The saloon bar gallantry of referring to a wife as 'the better half', while a proof of the unconscious persistence of long-forgotten myth, is usually tinged with irony. The soft-focus of courtship is soon replaced by hard-edged detail: the hair in the ears, the tuneless whistling, the sagging flesh. 'Romance!' says one of Alan Bennett's characters to her ageing spouse, 'You're asleep before the teeth hit the bottom of the glass!'

We need, however, most of us, to believe in the concept of eternal love. The arts, at every level, fulfil that need in part. Resurrected like ghosts for each succeeding generation, the fictitious lovers act out their troth. Yet it's not enough. The curtain comes down, the credit titles come up, we finish the novel, the bemedalled attendant declares the gallery about to close. We want the reassurance of the real. We demand creatures of flesh and blood, historical paramours, the great lovers.

Here though there is a further problem. Historical figures, as we do, age. In my adolescence I once bought, in an Oxford bookshop, a small engraving soon lost and much regretted. It showed three old crones with thin hair, warts, shrivelled breasts, dewlaps and toothless mouths. Beneath, in elegant seventeenth century calligraphy, they were identified. 'Cleopatra, Helen of Troy, The Queen of Sheba'. Even today, when 'vanity surgery' can remove folds of skin, inject silicone, flatten stomachs and restore a grotesque parody of youth, the years hold the cards. It's still a shock when the chat-show host introduces a goddess of one's formative adolescence and, down the staircase with arthritic caution, a painted old woman descends to shatter our illusions. Old age can be beautiful. Those who accept it move us. They acknowledge death as ever present, they look back, all passion

4

spent, at what they were, they present us with an exemplar; an encouraging model of how to make our inevitable exit with dignity. But those who ignore Hamlet's advice, who 'paint an inch thick', those induce panic, derision, or at best, pity.

I write of women, but this is not from male chauvinism. Men who refuse to recognise and accept their years react in a different if equally absurd way. They literally don't see themselves as they are. Those who resort to corsets and rouge form a small minority. Most imagine themselves still young, still irresistible. If rich and powerful they will find those willing to sustain their illusions, and vanity will help them believe they are loved for themselves alone. It's true no doubt that money, power and fame are powerful aphrodisiacs; that great beauty, even after it is gone, can sustain the imagination; that gerontophiles exist for whom wrinkles and the wounds of time are the ultimate turn on; that some, like Victor Hugo or Sarah Bernhardt, are the possessors of an individual chemistry which genuinely attracts lovers into their dotage. In general though the great lovers must remain either for ever young or more pertinently and characteristically in full vigour. We solve this paradox through their death. They die for us.

From Antony and Cleopatra to Benito Mussolini and Claretta Petacci a considerable proportion of Walter Dorin's couples died either together or shortly after one another. Through suicide, grief, provoked violence, they demonstrated what many artists and psychologists have always suspected or maintained; the close link between sex and death. It is death which alone preserves the illusion of unchanging love, which fixes the legend for ever. It is inconceivable to imagine Romeo and Juliet dawdling over a companionable breakfast in their fifties. Bonnie and Clyde were squalid little gangsters but, by dying together in a hail of police bullets, they entered our Valhalla. Many of the great lovers earned their place through a *partouse* with death.

Yet, despite Romeo and Juliet, extreme youth is not common amongst great lovers. The majority are on the edge of middle-age, and for a good reason. Obsessive passion demands the sacrifice of something positive. Love must be paid for and most young people haven't got enough for the ante. The best they can offer is to be cut off with a shilling, and even then there is a chance of reconciliation, usually with the appearance of the first grandchild. But children play a minimal role in the lives of the great lovers proper because they displace affection. If they exist at all they must be illegitimate or, if not, discarded. Marriage, on the other hand, isn't totally ruled out but it should have left in its wake at least one deserted and blameless spouse and, frequently, confused and unhappy children. Many an Octavia weeps, red-eyed, for Antony. Frieda Lawrence delivers her daughters to their paternal grandparents on the eve of her departure with D.H. They are 'blind and blank with pain'. Nothing: custom, compassion, good sense, material advantage, fear of social ostracism, the advice of friends, the weighing up of consequences, must count for anything. Love, in this sense, is a form of madness.

'L'Amour Fou!' The Surrealists named it and, with their passionate desire to change life, they elevated it into the equivalent of the transubstantiation of the Host. If there is a text book illustration of this ecstatic belief it is Luis Buñuel's film 'L'Age

5

d'Or'. Here two lovers—she the daughter of a high-ranking diplomat, he an important official in an international humanitarian organisation—are prepared to pay any price to satisfy the mutual need for erotic delirium. Rolling together in the mud at the laying of a foundation stone, they are prised apart—he frogmarched off by plainclothes policemen, she led away by nuns. Told by the head of the organisation over the telephone of the dire consequences of his obsession, a violent curse transports the old gentleman, chaining him, dead, to the ceiling. Images of onanism, scatology and sado-masochism abound. At one point, his face streaming blood, his hand deformed into a caressing stump, his eyes rolling in orgasmic ecstasy, the hero whispers to his adoring paramour: 'How happy we are since we murdered our children.' The fact that, like Lady Macbeth, they have no children is immaterial. It demonstrates how far—that is all the way—they are prepared to go.

Nevertheless Buñuel is too wise to allow his lovers to triumph. His film is a monument to frustration. The authorities intervene. The garden chairs are unsuitable for love-making. The girl, suddenly and arbitrarily, transfers her unsatisfied desires to a bearded old man in white tie and tails. Their sacrifice is in vain. The world has won and will, in the end, always win until it is destroyed and reborn with 'the marvellous' at its centre. Sexual irregularity tempered with discretion, casual promiscuity, 'a bit on the side', divorce and remarriage; all these can be accommodated, but put 'l'amour fou' up against the world, throw love in the face of the rational which is its enemy and ranks will close, the door crash shut, the sacrifice be demanded and paid.

The great lovers in this book fall into several categories: the Royal, the Powerful, the Deviant, the Criminal. Love in itself is not enough to qualify inclusion. No doubt there have been many amorous equivalents of Gray's village Hampdens and mute inglorious Miltons who behaved as extravagantly, as madly, as any here depicted but they were known only to their neighbours, famous at most within a day's ride or the environs of a suburb. How many Catherines and Heathcliffs went to their graves unrecorded by a Brontë? To qualify as a great lover it is necessary to 'kiss away Kingdoms and Provinces', to prove a 'triple pillar of the world transformed into a strumpet's fool'.

Royalty is fool-proof great lover material largely because it is allowed considerable licence as long as the rules are observed, and it needs considerable and foolhardy persistence to blow it. It was suggested to Edward VIII for instance that he could have his cake and eat it as long as he did so in private, but he wouldn't. His obsession insisted on abdication and a lifetime of exile with the Duchess. His grandfather was more realistic, his great-grandmother curiously enough, although nothing was ever proved, less so.

Great men, especially politicians and writers, can behave with amazing rashness. Admittedly some escape public whipping during their lifetime only to be exposed posthumously by the scavengers of archives and letters. The time bombs tick away in files and trunks. The academic voyeurs reconstruct, in volume after volume, every sigh, every stirring of erectile tissue. Encased in a velvet-lined box Napoleon's member goes under the hammer in a famous auction house.

For those without fame, power or privilege, only crime, which in itself is a form of power, can raise lovers to a legendary status. Crime breaks our rules and, when it is combined with *folie à deux*, we react with prurient fascination suggestive of suppressed envy. Murder for love elevated the meek and nondescript Dr Crippen into a bemused folk hero. Zola's 'Thérèse Raquin' expresses a powerful and universal dream. Great love is frequently stained with blood. If not of those who would frustrate it, then of the lovers themselves. If not of both protagonists then of the survivor who is deserted, betrayed or bereaved. Venus to her prey attached can prove as implacable as the female praying mantis who consumes her male alive during the very act.

Walter Dorin's pictures of these sacred monsters are an austere and humorous corrective to our over-excitable feelings. Solidly-built, painted in cool colours under grey skies or in sober and well-dusted interiors, his great lovers face us as if from the pages of a family album. A rather curious album perhaps because the artist, for all his restraint, is well aware that love is, after all, expressed through eroticism. I know nothing of Dorin's own obsessions but would imagine, on the evidence he provides that, for him, the thigh exposed between stocking top and knicker is a special interest (as well as a proof that he is not in his first youth), and that he is not unaffected by bare breasts. Yet here are no Dalian writhings, no hysterical romantic gestures. Even his suicides are committed with a certain calm. The tone is detached, almost cosy. Everything is conducted as in a well-run *maison tolérée* in a French provincial town in the last century.

The tragedy of great love is after all the fault of those of us who deny it. In a world that was prepared to recognise desire as central instead of locking it away in the dungeons of the unconscious or of castrating it with trivial pornography; in a time which could accept sexual ecstasy as a conformation of our nature rather than its flaw, we would need no 'Great Lovers' to expiate our guilt. Walter Dorin's pictures present his subjects as sane and us, as we hand out medals for crimes committed without passion, as mad. He teaches us a salutary lesson.

GEORGE MELLY

Edward, Prince of Wales
and
Lillie Langtry

'Tum Tum' to his friends, although never to his face, Edward, longtime Prince of Wales, for a mere decade King, turned his frustrated energy, denied a constructive outlet by his mother, to gluttony, gaming and lechery.

Married to Alexandra, a deaf Danish Princess whose understanding enabled her to send for Mrs Keppel, her husband's last mistress, to attend his deathbed, Edward pursued a series of affairs frequently consummated at the great country house parties of the period where, at dawn, the corridors were a-creak with portly gentlemen returning to their own bedrooms.

Edward's initiation into sex was at the instigation of his fellow officers in the Grenadier Guards at Curragh in Ireland where the Prince of Wales was stationed during the long vacation from Oxford. Their choice was an actress, or so she described herself, a girl named Nellie Clifton. Declaring herself agreeable, she was smuggled in to the General's quarters which had been placed at Edward's disposal during his stay and that would have been that. News, however, reached his appalled parents and, as Albert died only a few weeks later, the Queen never forgave her son for darkening his last days and, on this account, excluded him from all responsibility, thus opening the way to endless self-indulgence. Even when he was over fifty he was still snubbed and snapped at by his unforgiving mother; a fate he bore with remarkable patience and good humour.

Lillie Langtry was his mistress for only a few years in the 1870s and 1880s. She was born in Jersey, the daughter of the island's Dean, in 1853 and, at 21, married Edward Langtry, a wealthy Irishman. Acclaimed a great beauty, nicknamed 'The Jersey Lily', the result of a portrait of her so entitled by Millais, she first met, and enchanted, the Prince at a dinner party in 1877. Usually circumspect, although frequently dogged by scandal, his infatuation with her led him into reckless indiscretion, riding openly in her carriage or cantering by her side in Rotten Row. His wife accepted the situation, acting as though Mrs Langtry was as much her friend as his. Not so the wronged husband who scorned the frequently accepted role as *mari complaisant*, but his furious rages were powerless to force her to relinquish her glamorous role as mistress of the Prince of Wales.

The exact cause of the cooling of their relationship is uncertain. Some say it was her use of a pet name in public which effected the breach for he was ever a stickler for protocol; others her decision, unheard of for a society woman in those days, to

8

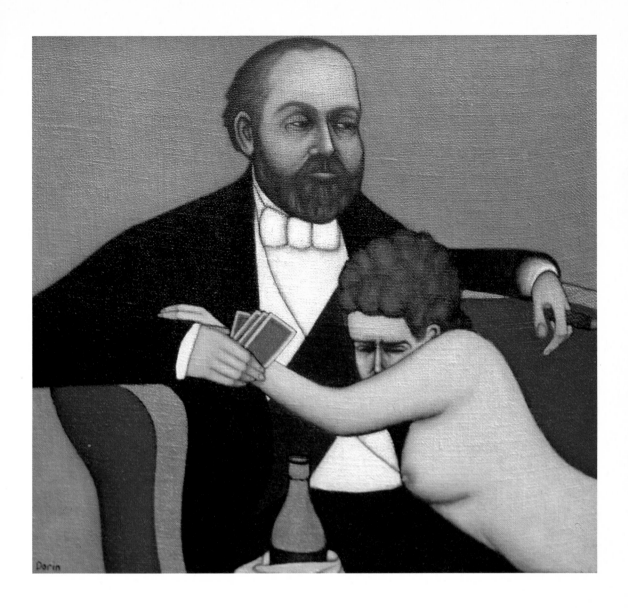

become an actress, her success less dependent on her skill as on the audience's knowledge of her Royal connections. On a return from a tour of America she found herself replaced by Daisy, Countess of Warwick.

Nevertheless her sexual 'By Appointment' led to other prominent liaisons and, after the death of her husband, another 'good' marriage. She died, suitably, in Monte Carlo in 1929.

Solomon
and
the Queen of Sheba

'So-o-o-o-o-o-o-o-o-lomon, he had 10,000 wives', sang Miss Elisabeth Welch, although the first book of Kings puts the number at somewhat lower, 700 plus 300 concubines.

Solomon was renowned for his wisdom, and was certainly an astute commercial administrator. He was helped in this by the fact that his reign was untroubled by war, mainly because his bellicose neighbours, Egypt and Assyria, were in a state of exhausted disarray.

His father had left him a considerable kingdom extending from Homs in the north to the Gulf of Aqaba in the south and Solomon forged several alliances which enabled him to exploit this favourable situation to the full. Like a lot of rich men he was not without ostentation. He spared no expense on the Temple and showed no desire to compete with the lilies of the field. He was also a committed lover. 'The Song of Solomon' is one of the greatest erotic love poems of all time.

The visit of the Queen of Sheba was probably a commercial move intended to establish trade relations with the Shebans. There was a great deal of feasting and fun. Nor had she come empty-handed. Her huge caravan was loaded with gold, precious stones and spices. They understood each other very well.

Whether they went to bed together before she returned home is in the realm of legend. Certainly if she was beautiful and willing it's very possible that Solomon, with his track record, would have felt this to be an agreeable way of ratifying the agreement and saying thank you for all the gold, precious stones and spices. The Bible emphasises the commercial advantages brought by the visit, but the Ethiopian 'Kebra Nagast' (Glory of the Kings) claims that she bore Solomon a son who became the first Lion of Judah, a tradition which emphasises the close ties which existed in antiquity between South Arabia and East Africa.

If Solomon did indeed father a child of the Queen it was something of a fluke. Despite his enormous harem, the Bible, which ignores any question of a Sheban by-blow, allows him only one son, Rehoboam, and later rabbinical commentators interpreted this as God's displeasure of the King's violation of monogamy, a rather absurd notion as God had failed to make his views on the subject known at that period.

There is to this day a tribe of Black Jews in Ethiopia, known as Falashes, which has been there since ancient times and claims to be descended from the Queen of Sheba's son.

11

David Lloyd George
✦ and ✦
Frances Stevenson

Over and over again one finds political ambition running between the shafts alongside a strong sexual drive. David Lloyd George is a case in point. He had the habit of pouncing in hansom cabs; long hair and cloak billowing out behind him. Nor were the wives of his parliamentary or cabinet colleagues safe. He is believed to number among his conquests the wife of Philip Snowden, the crippled Labour M.P. But the love of his life was Frances Stevenson, a clever graduate in classics who first entered his life when she was employed as a coach for his daughter Megan during the summer holidays of 1911. She was almost a prototype of the 'new woman' to be found in the works of Shaw and Wells, and in 1912 Lloyd George invited her to become a secretary at the treasury 'on his own terms'; these, as he made clear with a certain verbal delicacy, being 'in direct conflict with my essentially Victorian upbringing'. That Christmas she accepted and in February of 1913 they were, as she chose to call it, married, although the legal ratification of this state was delayed until after the death of Lloyd George's wife, Margaret, in 1943.

Lloyd George was a mass of contradictions; adept at political intrigue he was equally a man of genuine feeling for the weak and inadequate, laying the foundations of what was to become the Welfare State. He was certainly a man of great courage; one of the few to speak out, in opposition to the Liberal Party leadership, against the Boer War, a stand which cost him much and even put his life in some danger. During the 1914-18 war on the other hand, his feelings were bellicose. He drove out Asquith, rather as Churchill was to supplant Chamberlain some thirty years later, and a case can be made that without this move the war would have dragged on much longer, more lives would have been lost and the conclusion conceivably reversed. Equally it may be argued that his determination after the armistice to carry on the coalition with himself at its head succeeded in wrecking the Liberal Party. In 1922, through a stratagem designed by Baldwin and Lord Beaverbrook, Lloyd George was deposed and driven out for ever into the political wilderness. Yet, despite some early interest in the doctrines of Fascism, he was an early and fearless opponent of both Mussolini and Hitler. Lloyd George was created an Earl in 1945, an extraordinarily late acknowledgment of his service to the state, and he died later in that year.

His love for Frances Stevenson was of course proven, but even here there were traces of that deviousness which was part of his character. Initially she remained friendly with his wife and family, even sharing a bedroom with his daughter Megan when attending the Paris peace conference in 1918; but once it was recognised that

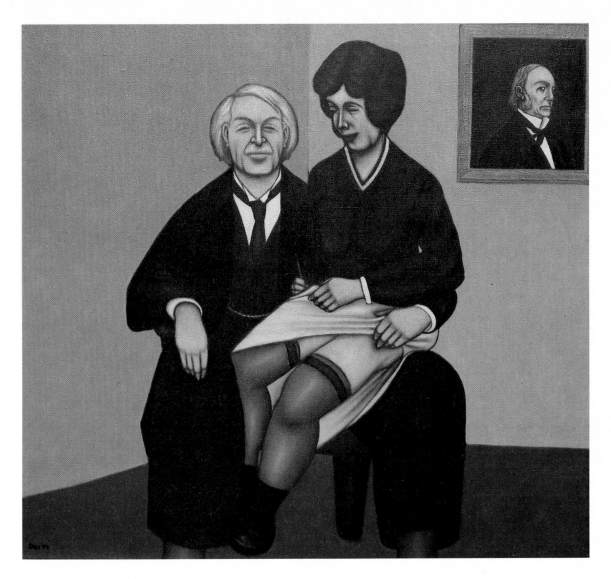

she had become a serious and permanent part of his life, a rift opened. She lived with her parents until 1915 but then set up in a flat of her own in London. In 1931 she moved to Worplesden near Churt, later building her own house near the Churt estate. It was called 'Avalon', and Lloyd George divided his time between visiting her there and acting as paterfamilias at Criccieth in North Wales. When with Frances or by letter, he would complain constantly about his family, no doubt to her satisfaction, but there is some evidence that he was not actually all that discontented in his other role. He did, however, marry her as soon as he was free, and she died, his dowager Countess, in 1972. His pet name for her was 'Pussy'.

13

Tristram
and
Iseult the Fair
(or Tristan and Isolde)

Wagner's opera is a much simplified version of the Arthurian story; a tale of treachery, single combat, poisoned weapons, sorcery, love philters and madness played out between Britain and Ireland a century after the Roman legions left.

After a traumatic childhood Tristram persuaded his father to allow him to serve his uncle Mark, King of Cornwall, a thoroughly evil creature for whom he had a totally misplaced loyalty. His first task was to take on, in single combat, Sir Marhaus, the Queen of Ireland's brother; a compromise accepted by the Irish King in lieu of a tribute which King Mark was unable or unwilling to pay. Tristram, although wounded by Sir Marhaus's illicitly poisoned spear, proved the victor, but the wound would not heal. As the only antidote was in Ireland, Tristram went there, prudently renaming himself 'Sir Tramtrist', as he imagined, correctly, that the Irish Queen might bear a grudge against the man who killed her brother.

The wound was healed through the ministrations of the Irish King's daughter, the beautiful Iseult, who fell in love with Tristram and he with her, but the Queen discovered Tristram's identity and the King advised his immediate departure.

Back home he was soon in more trouble. Both he and King Mark fancied the wife of a Baron but she favoured Tristram. King Mark tried to murder his nephew but only wounded him. At Mark's instigation, the wronged Baron tried to finish Tristram off but was slain in his turn despite Tristram's handicap.

Tristram prudently moved to Camelot to serve the more reliable King Arthur. He too was in trouble with the Irish and Tristram championed him through his superiority in single combat. The King and Tristram went together to Ireland where Arthur offered his knight whatsoever he desired. Tristram, idiotically, asked for the hand of Iseult, not for himself but for his uncle Mark, to whom he had pledged this service. Arthur reluctantly agreed.

The doomed pair sail for Cornwall. King Mark and Iseult are married but her passion for Tristram is not to be denied. They become lovers, flee, are recaptured, and after a series of frightful disasters and some months of happiness under the protection of Sir Lancelot, King Mark finally succeeds in killing Tristram by stabbing him in the back. Iseult falls prostrate on her lover's grave and dies of grief.

Wagner's simplification of this complicated tale was necessary. Had he followed every twist and turn (and I have only scratched the surface), there would have been no time for anyone to sing a note. As it is, at the very mention of Tristan and Isolde, the sweet anguish of Wagner's passionate equation of sex and death floods the mind with its insidious temptations.

Chopin
❧ and ❧
George Sand

Frédéric Chopin was half French. His father had emigrated to Poland in 1787 twenty-three years before the composer was born. An infant prodigy, he first played in public at the age of eight. After training at the Warsaw Conservatory and having some success in Poland and Germany he settled in Paris and, after a triumphant first concert in 1832, became a notable figure in the musical life of the French capital. Nevertheless he was, probably due to his always frail health, something of a recluse. The smell of a cigarette made him sick, a single glass of wine, drunk. Despite his passion for a free and independent Poland, he had no respect for mankind *en masse* and even his love for women was without passion. Yet his music, whether fiery or melancholy, was resolutely romantic. He was small, vain, proud and of a pallid beauty.

He met George Sand in 1838 and, almost immediately, accompanied her on a journey to Majorca which helped to undermine his already precarious health and exaggerate his consumption. They had a miserable time there. Doctors descended on him like vultures. When they had at last found a villa the authorities ordered him to leave the town for fear of spreading infection and then insisted on repapering all the walls at his expense. The lovers were forced to spend the rest of their stay in a Carthusian monastery.

George Sand was of a very different temperament from her tubercular genius. Balzac wrote of her, 'She is a bachelor, she is an artist, she is big, generous, loyal . . . morally she is a man of twenty.' She was born in Paris in 1804. Her father was an officer, her mother a milliner. The father died when she was very young and she was for the most part brought up by her grandmother, Madame Dupin, at Nohant in Berri on a property she was to inherit.

She was married at 18, to the illegitimate son of a Colonel, one Baron Dudevant. They had two children, Maurice and Solange. After nine years they parted amicably and, assuming the name of Sand, she set off to Paris to become a writer. She frequented Bohemian circles and took to dressing like a man, an eccentricity which caused a considerable stir. Among other lovers, before she met Chopin, was the great poet Alfred de Musset.

In effect, then, George Sand and Chopin were a considerable contrast; she, 'big, generous, loyal', the very spirit of life, he, sickly, reclusive, difficult, the walking advertisement of his inevitable death. They were not lovers for long, but remained companions, spending much of the time at Nohant, the happiest years of Chopin's short life, and it was there he composed much of his best music.

By 1846 two clouds appeared on the horizon in the shape of George Sand's difficult and treacherous children, now grown-up after their rackety and disorientating childhood. Maurice loathed Chopin and made his opinion clear, but it was his sister who caused the rift. She had married a sculptor called Clésinger and they had quarrelled with her brother and mother and recruited Chopin to take their part. George Sand, feeling herself the victim of a plot, and finding Chopin obstinate and intransigent about the affair, made no serious attempt at a reconciliation.

From there it was downhill all the way. He composed no more, but gave a series of exhausting concerts in England and Scotland. He returned to Paris in 1848 and died the following year. A monument by George Sand's son-in-law was erected over his grave, and at the unveiling a cup of Polish earth was strewn there. George Sand lived on until 1876, her work extending to one hundred volumes covering every literary genre.

Dr Crippen
❧ and ❧
Ethel Le Neve

Many men have murdered their wives and been forgotten, and it was undoubtedly the fact that he was the first murderer to be apprehended through the medium of wireless that gave Crippen his waxen immortality.

Dr Crippen was American, born in Michigan in 1862. He fell in love with a 17-year-old girl in New York, and although she was already the mistress of another man, married her. Cora Turner was vain, raucous, strongwilled and insatiably promiscuous but Crippen initially worshipped her.

Wishing to become an opera singer she left him in Philadelphia, where they were living, to train in New York. In 1900 he emigrated to England to become advertising manager for Munyan's Patent Medicines. Soon after, convinced now that her talent lay in the music hall, Cora joined him, calling herself 'Belle Elmore'. Only one professional engagement is recorded and that as a blackleg during a strike when she was booed off the stage, but she surrounded herself with spongers and sycophants prepared to pretend belief in her invented 'triumphs' in exchange for her husband's food and drink and, in the case of the more personable males, to go to bed with her as well. She, on the other hand, was ferociously jealous of him. He appeared to accept the situation but then, as we know, one day he poisoned her, calmly dismembered her and shortly afterwards fled.

Crippen had met Ethel Le Neve about 1904 when she came to work as a typist at his firm. She was the reverse of Cora; quiet, respectful and devoted to him. Why didn't he leave or divorce his wife? I suspect it was a passion for respectability; the cause of so many Victorian and Edwardian murders. Crippen might well have got away with it. It's true that Belle's friends, suspicious at her absence, went to the police, but he managed to persuade them that his wife had left him to return to an American lover, and the fact that he had told her circle a different story to save his face appeared more rather than less credible. Had he stayed put, this homicidal Pooter, Cora might have seeped beyond recognition into the sour earth of N.W.1.

Even after her remains, 'a mass of flesh', were uncovered in the Cellar of 39 Hilldrop Crescent, he could well have escaped if he and Ethel had sailed as man and wife under an assumed name. What madness, what compelling fantasy made him insist she dress as an unlikely-looking boy? And what of the quiet and mousy Le Neve? How much did she know or suspect of her 'father's' deed as, beneath the curious eye of Captain Kendal, she 'immoderately' squeezed his hand? She lived until the 1950s. She never married.

18

Lord Nelson
❧ and ❧
Lady Hamilton

Emma, Lady Hamilton, née Lyon, was a proof that given exceptional looks, native intelligence and determination, it is possible for a woman of however humble a background to ascend to any heights. Her life, with its sad end, demonstrates equally, the danger of relying on the love of a great man in a dangerous profession. During his lifetime the world fawns. After his death it hounds.

She was born the daughter of a labourer, at Preston, Lancashire about 1761. Her father died when she was still a child and her mother returned to her native Flintshire where her family were coal-miners.

At sixteen, already a beauty, Emma made her way to London where she became a domestic, first to a physician, later to a tradesman.

Fate can seem a conspirator at times. Emma received a letter from home informing her that one of her relations had been seized by the Naval press-gang and asking her if she could plead his cause at the Admiralty. Not only did she succeed, but she became the mistress of the officer she spoke to, a Captain, later Admiral, Payne and, once established in this profession, passed on to Sir Harry Featherstonehaugh and then to the Hon. Charles Greville.

Greville also presented her to his uncle, Sir William Hamilton, the British ambassador in Naples, and it was he who eventually married her in 1791. She was not received at Court; Queen Charlotte was a little less flexible than the rest of the fashionable intelligence, but this didn't worry her especially. She had not after all done badly for the daughter of a Lancashire labourer.

Returning to Naples with her elderly husband and bearing, it is said, a letter of introduction to its Queen from Marie Antoinette, she soon established herself as a considerable diplomat in her own right, doing much to influence the Neapolitan Royal Family in the British interest during the war with post-revolutionary France.

It was she, when her husband had failed with the King, who persuaded the Queen to allow Nelson to provision in Naples in contravention of an agreement with the French, and she collaborated with him yet again in effecting the escape of the Royal Family to Palermo during a Jacobin revolution which Nelson was instrumental in suppressing.

Naturally enough these events brought Nelson and Emma Hamilton together, and friendship and gratitude turned into love and infatuation. Nelson was already married to a doctor's widow, a union he had described as based on 'affection and prudence'. This was not to last. Sir William Hamilton may have been prepared to act the *mari complaisant* to the one-eyed, one-armed national hero, but Lady Nelson was less obliging and when her husband's relationship with Emma became public

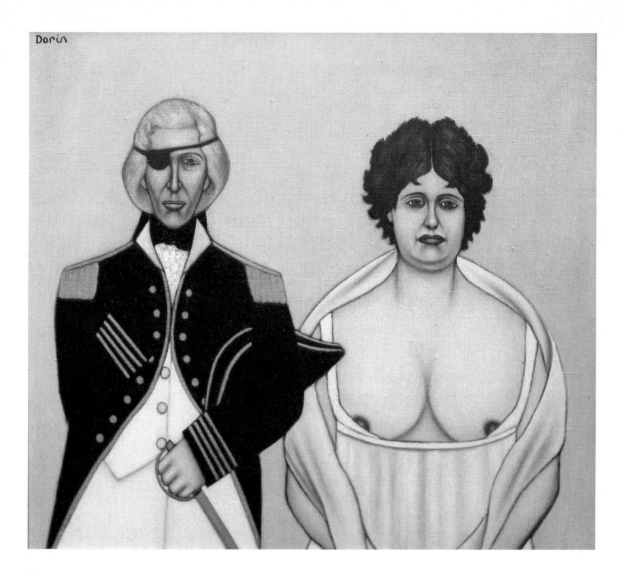

Dorin

knowledge they were separated.

Nelson, for the rest of his life, wrote three letters to Emma every day when they were apart. There was a child, Horatia, which Lady Hamilton claimed to be his and he also acknowledged. Sir William Hamilton died before Nelson but, with his own wife still living, there was no question of marriage. On the eve of Trafalgar, the Admiral added a codicil to his will leaving Lady Hamilton as 'a legacy to my King and Country'. Neither King nor Country accepted the charge. Tears were wept and monuments erected to Nelson, but the woman he loved with all his heart was left without property or income, was imprisoned for debt and then fled with their child to Calais, where eighteen months later, in great privation, she died.

Scott and Zelda Fitzgerald

'I lost my capacity for hoping on the little roads that led to Zelda's sanatorium.' So wrote Scott Fitzgerald of his wife's madness; a state which first manifested itself towards the end of the 1920s when she began to practise ballet both by day and night, and he to drink with increasing regularity, his vogue over, only the hopeless years as a drunken Hollywood hack ahead.

One of the century's great writers, while almost forgotten by his death in 1940, his place is now secure. Much of his work is marred or inconclusive but all of it is touched by genius and, in *The Great Gatsby*, he created a flawless masterpiece. A mass of insecurity, bedazzled by the idea of the rich, he was obsessed with perfection, prepared to redraft everything over and over again. He was sensitive and charming when sober, difficult and dismissive when drunk.

Despite his precariously middle class family's shaky finances, he was sent to a fashionable private school, then on to Newman and Princeton. There he rubbed shoulders with money, observing closely those able to spend it with casual style.

'The rich are different from us, Ernest,' said Scott Fitzgerald.

'Yes,' growled Hemingway. 'They have more money.'

In 1917, while in the army and stationed in Alabama, he fell in love with Zelda Sayre, the daughter of a judge but, confirming all his doubts, was refused permission to marry her. Her family made it clear he would be unable to support her in the style that they and she expected.

He had, however, begun to write his first novel, *This Side of Paradise*. It appeared, after much revision, in 1920 and made him famous. Money poured in, enough to renew his courtship, this time successfully. The Fitzgeralds moved to Paris where life during those pre-depression years seemed, as Hemingway was to call it later, 'a moveable feast'. The Fitzgeralds had everything: beauty, charm, success. Their friend, Ring Lardner, called them 'the Prince and Princess of their generation'. Then came Zelda's madness, the failure of *Tender is the Night*, the increasing reliance on the bottle. The party was over.

Zelda's attacks hardened into permanency. Fitzgerald went to Hollywood, sustained only by the selfless devotion of the movie columnist, Sheila Graham. By the time he died of a massive heart-attack in 1940, he must have thought of himself as a complete failure. The reassessment came too late.

From 1936 Zelda, from whom he had become estranged, was a patient at the Highland Hospital, Ashville, North Carolina. In 1948 there was a fire and she was among the dead, identifiable only by a charred slipper lying beneath her body.

Queen Victoria ❧ and ❧ John Brown

The death of her beloved Albert in 1862 drove his wife, Queen Victoria, temporarily mad and, for a very long period afterwards turned her into a recluse. Whose idea it was that it might cheer her during the first few desperate months after her loss to bring down from the Highlands her favourite pony, Lochnayer, and have it led into her presence by her head gillie, John Brown, is no longer known, but it was an imaginative stroke and much appreciated. Brown had been hired, as a young man, by Albert personally and had been devoted to him. Brown was a direct link, a living reminder of those happy and carefree holidays at Balmoral and although, having delivered Lochnayer, he returned immediately to Scotland, a few years later she sent for him to come down to Windsor as her personal servant.

He remained in this position until his death in 1883 and a great deal of speculation and gossip surrounded him, especially during his early years of service. The Queen, so severe, so daunting towards anyone, even her ministers, allowed this blunt, rough and frequently drunken Highlander amazing liberties. He addressed her as 'woman', bullied and chided her for neglecting her health and was extremely short, not to say impertinent, to anyone, however distinguished, who didn't meet with his approval in their treatment of his mistress or in their respect to him.

She, for her part, praised him to everybody in the most extravagant terms. He was for her, she claimed, so many things: stable lad, valet, page, even 'maid servant' because 'he is so good with shawls'. Husband too? It was hardly surprising that those who didn't care for him, and especially the high-born ladies of that dull court whom he treated with such off-hand rudeness, should have chosen to speculate along this line, and there were even rumours of a secret marriage.

But were they lovers? It's impossible to establish it either way although certainly the letters from her worldly Private Secretary to his wife were destroyed by someone, possibly Princess Beatrice, the Queen's youngest daughter, and it was she who thought fit to edit and, in some passages, rewrite her mother's memoirs.

Of all the many people who disliked or hated the gillie there is no doubt that the middle-aged, much put-upon Prince of Wales headed the list. When the Queen herself eventually died one of the first actions of the new monarch was to smash, break, burn or otherwise destroy all the innumerable souvenirs of the hated John Brown at Windsor Castle. There is no doubt that, whether physically or no, the Queen and her servant were emotionally extremely close and that the rejected and despised heir reacted with full oedipal resentment and rage to their relationship.

Mussolini
·➤🜲] and 🜲➤· Claretta Petacci

Benito Mussolini (b.1883, shot 1945) while he was the first, was by no means the worst of the 20th-century dictators. His absurd egomania, despite its unpleasant and at times fatal side-effects, was closer to comic rather than grand opera.

In sexual matters Mussolini was an insatiable, wham-bam-thank-you-ma'm male chauvinist pig. He liked all women providing they were not too thin, and had a fetishistic obsession with smell: sweat for choice or, if that was not present, pungent scent. He himself had no love of hygiene resorting, as often as not, to Cologne rather than soap and water. Like Byron, he usually rejected bed, with its implied tenderness and intimacy, for the nearest flat surface, the floor or the edge of a desk.

Nevertheless he was not incapable of love. In 1909, while still a socialist agitator, he lived for a time in great poverty with a 16-year-old girl, the younger daughter of his father's mistress; but the great love of his life was Claretta Petacci whom he met in 1936 when he was 53 and she 24.

It was by no means a popular liaison. Count Ciano, the Duce's son-in-law, said that whereas there would have been no objection to troops of mistresses, the Duce's infatuation with one alone was 'a serious scandal'. This was not because of their sexual relationship, but the result of Claretta's nepotism. The Petacci family infiltrated everywhere. Her brother, Marcello, made a fortune by smuggling gold through the diplomatic bag, trading in foreign currency and placing contracts and arranging profitable appointments. Her father, a physician, was made the medical correspondent on a newspaper, *Il Messaggero*. Her sister Miriam was helped towards a successful film career. Some of these appointments were acceptable—Dr Petacci was after all a distinguished physician, Miriam a competent actress. Marcello's venality was not, nor was the elevation of the 26-year-old Aldo Viduseoni, a close friend of the Petaccis, to the secretaryship of the Fascist Party. Not for the first or last time, love sabotaged prudence, blinded its hostage to all considerations beyond the happiness of his obsession, transformed a beast into a slave.

Mussolini's jackal-like opportunism in entering the war led to his downfall. A case can also be made out that the admirable military incompetence of the Duce's generals was a vital contribution to the Führer's defeat. With Italy falling enthusiastically to the allies, Mussolini was rescued from internment and, at Hitler's orders, reluctantly installed as the puppet ruler of German-occupied Italy. His family and Claretta joined him. The farce was played out to its conclusion. Sick and mad, he spent much of his time playing the violin and then, when capture became

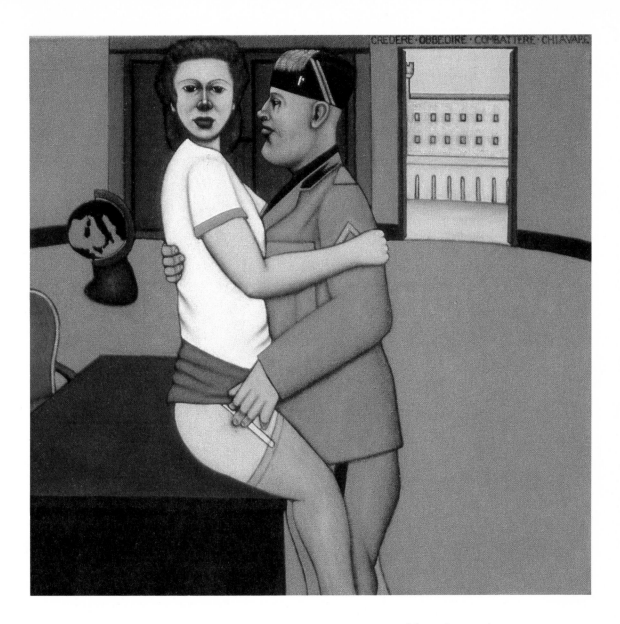

inevitable, tried to effect his escape in a German convoy. Although wearing a German greatcoat he was recognised by the communist partisans who intercepted the convoy in a lonely place named, with absurd irony, Musso. Handed over to one Colonel Valerio, he and Claretta were executed and their bodies afterwards suspended from lamp posts for the benefit of news cameras. It is, however, uncertain if Claretta's death was intentional. It is rumoured that she was shot by accident, interposing her body in an attempt to save her lover.

Virginia Woolf
and
Victoria Sackville-West

'A Guard's officer in bearskin and breeches'. Virginia Woolf's description of the great love of her life, the patrician, author and gardener, Victoria Sackville-West. It was not especially a physical relationship although it is probable they went to bed together once or twice. There was, from Mrs Nicolson's point of view the worry of Mrs Woolf's attacks of insanity. Suppose she were to go mad in her arms?

For Virginia it seems to have been initially very much a school-girl crush. Vita's much self-advertised grand connections, the great house which had been in her family since 1586, the grandmother who was once a Spanish dancer; a heady mixture for the romantic and not a little snobbish Bloomsbury novelist. For Victoria too there was much to be gained. Virginia's near-platonic adoration was a considerable relief after the fiendish jealous physicality of her affair with the difficult and possessive Violet Trefusis.

It was not that Virginia especially admired Vita as a writer. Whatever her emotional attachment she preserved her aesthetic judgment with a detachment rare among the infatuated. She felt, although naturally enough she was careful never to let her know it, that Vita wrote with 'a pen of brass'. She was in love rather with her character, her virile beauty, her sense of adventure. Striding about on her long and beautiful legs, Victoria Sackville-West appeared to her like a Prince in a fairy story.

It was for her, and about her that she wrote *Orlando*, a fantasy in which a noble lad, born in 1586 lived until 1928, knowing everyone of note, ageing over this long period, a mere twenty years, and changing into a woman half-way through. It is a lyrical and fanciful love letter and for Virginia, for whom writing was a slow and agonising business, the easiest and most spontaneous book she ever wrote.

Platonic or no — 'It's a great thing being a eunuch as I am', she wrote to Vita in 1927 — there was no doubt that Virginia Woolf loved her Orlando obsessively. According to Quentin Bell, her sister's son and the principal chronicler of the Bloomsbury Group, 'Virginia felt as a lover felt — she desponded when she fancied herself neglected, despaired when Vita was away, waited anxiously for letters, needed Vita's company and lived in that strange mixture of elation and despair which lovers — and one would suppose only lovers — can experience.'

Vita's feelings are less clear-cut. For one thing she used many of her lesbian feelings to play games with the complicated emotional responses of her homosexual but jealous husband, Harold Nicolson. Even so she was comparatively reassuring where Virginia was concerned, at any rate on a physical level. 'One's

love for Virginia is a very different thing: a mental thing, a spiritual thing, if you like, an intellectual thing . . .'

Victoria Sackville-West was made a Companion of Honour in 1948 and died in 1962. Virginia Woolf, fearing another attack of her recurrent madness and believing her creative powers to be waning, drowned herself in a river in Sussex in 1941.

Frankie  and Johnnie

Their historical existence is non-proven, indeed in one version of the ballad they are named as Frankie and Albert, but they remain for all that a potent myth; the subject of a ballet, an animated cartoon, a favourite vehicle of Mae West's.

The reason for their survival when so many other bar-room ballads have either vanished or are known only to specialists, is that their story is both universal and rich in convincing and particularised detail. Johnnie, one presumes, is a pimp. Frankie, in the full version, buys him hundred dollar suits, but what she does to keep him is entirely different from what he does for his own pleasure. The jealous whore is not uncommon. Frankie looks over the transom to discover Johnnie *flagrante delicto*. He does her wrong in the arms of Nellie Bligh. She shoots him for it.

Are they white or black, this ill-starred pair? It's hard to say and depends largely on the singer, the interpretation. Where does the drama take place? It may have once been a frontier song, much added to, much amended. The electric chair in which Frankie pays the price is surely a later addition. In the old days she'd have been hanged.

They live near by, near to the saloon. Frankie goes there for a bucket of beer wearing only a kimono. The barman tells her where Johnnie is and with whom. She looks, she sees, she returns home to fetch her forty-four, she shoots him 'right through the bar-room door'.

> 'The first time she hit him he staggered
> The next time she hit him he fell
> The third time she hit him, Oh Lordy,
> There was a new man's face in hell.'

Dead. Yet the very next verse suggests that, as the way with ballads, another source may have yielded an effective verse in the face of logic. He cries:

> 'Roll me over easy
> Roll me over slow,
> Roll me over on the left side
> 'Cause your bullets hurt me so.'

Then she cries to be arrested, locked up, judged and executed. In one of Bessie Smith's blues there is a similar situation:

> 'The Judge said, "Bessie, why'd you kill your man?" (*twice*)
> I said, "Judge you ain't no woman and you don't understand" '

And Frankie's death as described is terrifying in its poetic simplicity.

30

'I saw Frankie one more time
She was sittin' in the 'lectric chair.
Waitin' to go and meet her God
With the sweat drippin' out of her hair.'

W.H. Auden, with good reason, included the full version in the *Oxford Book of Light Verse*. As a fable of jealousy and love it has never been bettered. Where ever and if ever Frankie went 'roóty-toot-toot', she and Johnnie earn their place here.

31

Dante
and
Beatrice

He was nine and she was eight. They were at a feast in the house of a banker called Folco de' Portinari. It was May Day 1274. From that moment on Beatrice de' Portinari was ever in his thoughts, his principal inspiration, his measure of excellence, the bridge between the temporal and the eternal.

Thirteenth and fourteenth century Italy required a giant to make sense of what was happening. Behind the poet the landscape was dominated by the great cathedral of medieval theology with its gargoyles and saints, in front of him the dawn of humanism waxed ever brighter, the voice of individualism challenging the pious incantations of the faceless faithful. It was Dante's immense task to encapsulate this passionate confrontation of faith and reason, this age of transition. The child of eight at a party grew up into a beautiful young woman. She became the focus of his erotic imagination which he struggled with and succeeded in sublimating and transforming into a fleshless spiritual being, a symbol of divine love; the word made flesh transmuted into the flesh made word.

It's impossible for us now to imagine what it must have been like to wake up to face a day in late thirteenth century Florence. Everything in front of our eyes — the bread on the kitchen table, a pigeon on the window ledge, the city with its bridges, the light on the Tuscan hills above — these were not only themselves but symbols of greater meaning. Yet at the same time politics were a dangerous game played out by individuals with passionate and personal intensity and Dante was in the thick of them. His convictions made him back all the wrong horses, his intransigence prevented him from compromise. In a quarrel involving two great Florentine families and the Papacy, Dante, then a magistrate, was made the scapegoat and exiled, vowing never to return without a complete recognition of his innocence. This was never to be granted, and he died in Ravenna in 1321.

Yet perhaps without this obligatory severance from his roots, and the vision of his beloved Beatrice ever before his eyes, he would never have written those extraordinary works in which reason, faith, cruelty and love, classicism and gothic scholarship, the past and the future are fused to create a divine incandescence. Of course the equation of lust and piety are not unique to Dante, and the whole suppression of sexuality by the church was and is surely an attempt to channel the force and energy thus deflected to other uses. In Dante's case certainly his obsession with his Beatrice gave him the key to his kingdom. News of her death almost destroyed him but then, in the end, he was dispossessed and married.

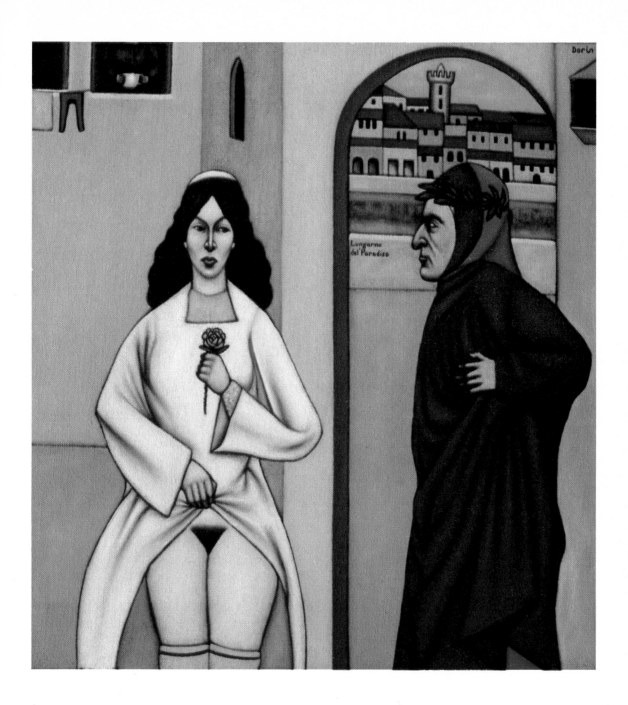

33

Napoleon ❦ and ❧ Josephine

Neither was truly French. Bonaparte was born in Corsica only a year and three months after its cession by the Genoese Republic, and besides that his family was of Tuscan origin, while Josephine was a Creole from Martinique. They met shortly after the French Revolution and were married in 1796.

Josephine, thirty-three at the time, had already lived a full and dangerous life. At fifteen she had been married, by arrangement, to Le Comte de Beauharnais, but, disliking each other intensely, they pursued in France their separate ways and eventually divorced. She returned to her birthplace.

When the political situation on the islands became threatening, Josephine sailed again for France and became reconciled to her husband (she was always skilled at reconciliations. She must have been quite extraordinarily attractive and manipulative). Their realignment was short-lived. They became embroiled in the Revolution and, as the Count was a constitutionalist, they were thrown into prison by Robespierre and the husband sent to the guillotine.

While still in jail Josephine became acquainted with Mme Tallien and, with the end of the Terror and their subsequent release, these two ladies became the Queens of the post-revolutionary salons, and, in Josephine's case, the mistress of Barras, a leading member of the Directory, and in effect, ruler of France.

Whether or not the affair was over, it was something of a step down to marry Napoleon even though he had been appointed commander of the Italian expedition of 1796-7. It is evident that she had a keen nose for the will to power, but equally she was the reverse of prudent or faithful. She neglected to answer her husband's passionate love letters from Italy and Egypt, and news of her many infidelities must have reached him by almost every post. He threatened to divorce her. However, not only did he forgive her and agree to repay her enormous debts but, in 1804, she was crowned Empress at his side.

Finally, though, her extravagance, her open adulteries and her inability to produce an heir led to a nullification. In order to effect a political marriage to Marie Louise, daughter of the Emperor of Austria, Napoleon broke the news to his wayward but much loved wife. This time her tears and reproaches were in vain. Although much affected, he stood firm, and in the end she gave her reluctant consent.

He left her to act out his tragic role. She was installed at the little court of Malmaison where she grew flowers and received the great of Europe. She died in 1814. Her funeral was attended, not only by the eminent, but also by thousands of

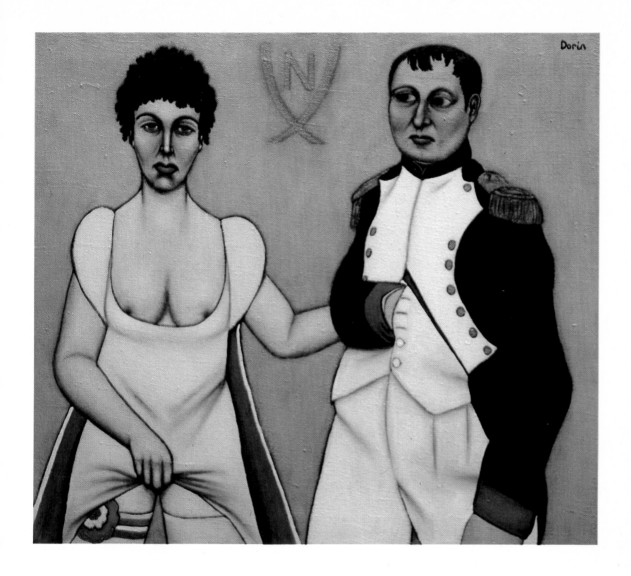

the poor whose love, for no reason beyond her remarkable charisma, she had won
and held. Napoleon was not present. He was in exile in Elba.

The mysterious attraction of this pleasure-loving, profligate, wayward woman is
evident by its effect on others — The Tsar of All The Russias was walking in her
gardens while she lay dying. Sexuality on this level is beyond mere beauty, it is an
irresistible force. Napoleon may never have said 'Not tonight Josephine', but it is
known that on his return to her after his campaigns he would send her a message in
advance. It read, 'Don't wash'.

35

King Carol of Rumania
and
Magda Lupescu

A true Ruritanian romance, the love of King Carol II of Rumania for Magda Lupescu burned with the brilliance of a magnesium flare in the dark night of the old Europe before the coming of the grey bureaucratic day.

The unruly son of King Ferdinand I, Carol, in 1921 married Helen, daughter of King Constantine of the Hellenes, a suitably politic match and she, on cue, presented him with an heir, Prince Michael.

Although the marriage was unhappy, the façade might have remained intact but for the Prince's meeting at a party with the wife of an army officer, the flaming red-haired, blue-eyed Magda, with whom he fell desperately in love.

Lupescu's origins are disputed but there is no doubt she had some Jewish blood and, in the mounting anti-semitism of the period, this was used to stir up feeling against the Prince. Far from seeking to suppress the scandal, the Palace fed the press with scandalous details about the liaison, constantly describing Lupescu as 'a red-haired Jewess, the daughter of a junk pedlar'.

The campaign succeeded. In 1925 Carol was forced to abdicate all right to the throne in favour of his infant son, a move confirmed by the will of his father, King Ferdinand, who died soon afterwards. The young Prince Michael was declared King under a Regency and Princess Helen was persuaded to divorce her husband to make sure the way was barred to his return. Some time before, Lupescu had been visited by the King's agents who had persuaded her to leave the country, threatening not only her personal safety but that of the Jewish community as a whole. She went to Paris where Carol soon joined her.

The Regency, however, proved unpopular, the Liberal Party was dismissed, and a National Peasant Government took over, inviting Carol to return from his exile in France and England. Offered a place in the Regency he refused and was crowned King in 1930. An attempt at a reconciliation with Helen proved a failure and a year later Magda Lupescu returned to join him.

In a desperate attempt to retain his throne, Carol declared a personal dictatorship but in 1940 it was overthrown. As they fled the country, their train was sprayed by Fascist bullets but, lying flat on the floor of their carriage, Carol and Magda were unhurt.

In Brazil, in 1947, informed by doctors that Magda was dying, King Carol married his true love, granting her the courtesy title of Princess Elena of Rumania. She recovered, however, and it was Carol who died first in 1953. Elena survived until 1977 to the approximate age of 81.

Oscar Wilde
and
Lord Alfred Douglas

That Oscar Wilde was infatuated with the arrogant, extravagant, treacherous, petulant and more than a little mad Lord Alfred Douglas is beyond dispute. Snobbery may have entered into it, but the boy's beauty held him in thrall and certainly a masochistic need to be bullied and exploited played its part. As to the physical expression of that love there are doubts as to whether anything took place. If it did, its duration was certainly brief. Both Oscar and Bosie preferred 'rough trade'. To quote Wilde's own Lady Bracknell on the more acceptable theme of finding husbands for unmarried daughters, they 'hunted together so to speak'.

Douglas's ferocious and mutual hatred of his father, the insane Marquis of Queensberry, was the cause of Wilde's downfall. Queensberry, heterosexual certainly but coarse and callous in his behaviour, pursued Wilde with mounting innuendoes and insults culminating in his leaving a note at the author's club, 'To Oscar Wilde posing as a somdomite' (*sic*). All Wilde's friends begged him to ignore it but Douglas, whose dream was to attack his father from the witness box, egged him on to sue for criminal libel. Not only did Wilde fail, but evidence produced by Queensberry's detectives led to his prosecution and eventual imprisonment. He had time to escape abroad, but perhaps from a taste for martyrdom, refused. From prison he reproached the 'lovely boy' in a long letter, 'De Profundis', but so great were his feelings that, despite the threat of the withdrawal of his wife's allowance, Wilde continued to see Bosie after his release and exile to France.

Wilde's love destroyed him. Douglas lived a long litigious life, his bureau full of photographs of himself as a beautiful youth which, in withered old age, he would press, unasked, on casual visitors.

Dorin

39

Bonnie
and
Clyde

Their legend would have died, was dead for most people until the movie, starring the beautiful Faye Dunaway and the handsome Warren Beatty, resurrected them as glamorous and engaging criminals who robbed banks with dedicated amateurism before dying in slow balletic motion with decidedly orgasmic effect.

'Bonnie and Clyde were very pretty people,' sang Georgie Fame and, while true of Dunaway and Beatty, in reality they were far less agreeable. Bonnie Parker was a tough ex-waitress, Clyde Barrow an aimless drifter. Both of them were Texans. She was born in 1909. He in 1911. Their meeting was fortuitous. They teamed up in the late 1920s at the beginning of the Depression and began, with growing dedication, to rob banks. During their five years of active partnership they killed eighteen people.

The equation the film proposed, and it was a popular thesis during the 1960s, is that capitalism is, by its nature, corrupt and in consequence the criminal is some kind of noble rebel whose own activities are, at the same time, a caricature of legalised capitalism and yet somehow a more defensible version of it. Bonnie and Clyde coincided with the Depression and so, *ipso facto*, they were presented as individuals who opposed it and, until shot down, overrode it.

In my view part of this argument holds water. The ruthless activity of the American robber barons with their murderous strike breakers and planted stool pigeons certainly accounted for misery and death on a far larger scale than the two lovers and their little gang of malcontents.

Their status as folk heroes is explicable. The Depression was blamed on the bankers because so many banks collapsed and with them hundreds of thousands of people's savings, but in reality the banks were just one link in the disaster.

Still, Bonnie and Clyde robbed banks, that is to say they robbed the robbers, and so won an amused admiration from the new-poor, the disinherited of the United States. They appealed therefore to the anarchic spirit which is another side of the American psyche. Even their nemesis was appropriate. Somebody squealed. An ambush was prepared. As though out of superstition, they were blasted almost to pieces.

Was Clyde impotent until he met Bonnie? The film suggested so, adding yet another facet to the beautification of two not especially endearing hoods. Should we be encouraged to weep for them and ignore their eighteen victims? It is characteristic of our times that we are invited to do so.

41

Antony
and
Cleopatra

Shakespeare has imposed his image of the pair of them. Impossible now to imagine them in any other way, but his Antony and Cleopatra are Elizabethans addressing us in those heart-breaking, memorable phrases at two removes. The facts are not inaccurate, but the emotions in the play are of another time, another place. Neither ours nor those of ancient Rome. We see the pair through Shakespeare's great, distorting glass.

They were both pagans: their gods amoral as themselves, differentiated from their worshippers only by their arbitrary powers. Human conduct measured itself against no ideal. The moralists of the pre-Christian world were truly heroic. What they proposed was its own reward.

Antony was always power-happy but betrayed by an equally strong appetite for dissipation and an aptitude for running up debts. Still he had a talent for backing the right horse, of being, in that small slow-moving world which was the whole world, in the right place at the right time. He stuck with Julius Caesar and Caesar paid off both before and after his assassination. It was a shrewd move marrying Octavia, Octavius's sister, thereby linking himself to his fellow triumvir, but then his luck ran out. He met and fell in love with Cleopatra. 'The triple pillar of the world transformed into a strumpet's fool.' The chilly Octavius, using his sister as the excuse for fulfilling his ambitions to become the sole ruler of Rome, made war. Antony, defeated, believing wrongly his love dead, committed suicide by falling on his sword. The reformed libertine in love is, like a convert to any faith, blind to all else.

Cleopatra on the other hand was, it would seem, many things. Of Macedonian origin, a descendant of one of the generals who had conquered Egypt under Alexander the Great, her family combined astonishing brutality with great love of learning and the arts. Under these cultural sadists Alexandria became the most dazzling city of antiquity.

She herself used her beauty and wit to her advantage. First the mistress of Julius Caesar, and bearing him a son called Caesarion, she had little trouble in seducing Antony when summoned before him at Philippi after the defeat of the conspirators.

After a winter in Egypt with her, he returned to Rome to marry Octavia, his last act of political self-interest, but Cleopatra had become an obsession, and he returned to her to 'kiss away kingdoms and provinces'.

D.H. Lawrence
and
Frieda von Richthofen

Genius or no, and the general opinion is that he was, everything I've heard or read about Lawrence confirms him to have been a frightful little shit. Hysterically malicious, disloyal, given to biting eventually any hand extended in friendship, one might have wished him, in theory, no worse fate than involvement with the Baroness Frieda von Richthofen, an idle, sluttish, arrogant lie-abed with whom he eloped in 1912. The strange aspect of this liaison of two seemingly unreconcilable nightmares was that their long, insolvent, peripatetic relationship with its violent quarrels and reconciliations suited them both perfectly, and it was always true of Lawrence that he needed an intense and difficult relationship (his mother; Jessie Chambers), in order to fuel his creative fire.

Lawrence: neat, orderly, fiercely monogamous and hard-working, roamed the world with this promiscuous, cunning, naive, obtuse creature until his death. Jealousy, albeit directed at different targets, would seem to have been the only quality they shared. She did all she could to prevent him working, resenting equally his determination to fulfil himself and equally his use of her as a source of fictional characters in almost all the novels and in many of his stories, while for his part, he was enraged by her open and casual infidelities and equally jealous of the three children of her marriage to an inoffensive academic, Ernest Weekley. Nevertheless he continued to write and she to put it about until death uncoupled them.

They surface frequently, and usually in conflict, in the memoirs of the period. Osbert Sitwell's mother, writing to her son from Italy, described an unsolicited visit from 'two friends of yours' (they were not to remain friends long. The suspicion that Osbert was the model for Lady Chatterley's impotent husband soon put paid to that). She described Lawrence as a talkative little man and Frieda as a large German woman who trailed behind them on a tour of the castle holding on to the bedposts and sighing deeply. She had, it was obvious, no idea who they were. On the other hand Harry Crosby, the rich American expatriate poet and eventual suicide knew very well. In Paris on one occasion during the late 1920s he played them Bessie Smith's recording of 'Empty bed blues', thinking that Lawrence might feel in sympathy with its open eroticism. In this he proved to be mistaken. D.H., in many ways puritanical, loathed Bessie's let-it-all-hang-out sensuality and concomitant humour but Frieda adored it, playing it over and over again until eventually Lawrence took the record off the turntable and broke it over her head. Yet the relationship held.

44

The books, immortalising the ungrateful baroness, were written, great lovers they remained and on Frieda's death in 1956, and at her express request, despite an intervening marriage to an Italian ex-officer, she was buried in Taos, New Mexico, a few feet from the Memorial Chapel which holds Lawrence's ashes.

Archduke Rudolf
❧ and ❧
Maria Vetsera
(Mayerling)

On the morning of 30 January 1889 one Loschek, valet to the Archduke Rudolf, unable, despite repeated knocking, to gain access to the room where, the night before, his master had retired with his young mistress Maria Vetsera, became alarmed, and ran to inform Count Hoyas, one of Rudolf's staff and a guest at the hunting lodge of Mayerling. With the arrival of the Archduke's brother-in-law, a decision was made to break down the door. A panel splintered and, gazing in horror through the jagged hole, the valet could make out the sprawling bodies of Rudolf and Maria. The Archduke had shot first her, and then himself through the right temple.

In many ways this would seem to be the ideal example to illustrate the concept of the great lovers. He was just over thirty: handsome, irresistible to women, of great promise. She, only seventeen and fresh from a convent, was of touching beauty. Unhappily married, frustrated by his father, the Emperor Franz Joseph, from initiating liberal reforms within the reactionary and repressive Austrian Empire, Rudolf had apparently chosen death with his beloved rather than a life of compromise and hypocrisy.

There are, however, political complications which suggest a put-up job. Rudolf's liberalism was an anathema to his father and, denied a political role, he sought out the company of liberals, intellectuals and Jews. While by no means a revolutionary, it was his intention to remodel the Hapsburg Empire on the French and British democratic system when his chance came, but it is very possible that his impatience had made him decide to jump the gun. The very night before the tragedy there had been an abortive uprising in Budapest and in the late afternoon Rudolf had received several mysterious visitors at the lodge and held them briefly in furtive but urgent conversation before their equally hurried departure. The Emperor's secret police were extremely efficient and there is no doubt that his son, with his suspect radical views, was under surveillance. An open arrest would have created great difficulties but it would have been simple, in this isolated setting, to have faked a mutual suicide. There are other theories too—an affair of honour over the Archduke's alleged seduction of the Countess Auersperg—but a judicious political assassination seems to be more likely.

For the world, however, the most simple explanation remains the most moving; the brilliant young aristocrat, the beautiful girl dying for love in a hunting lodge, hidden in the heart of the great forest with its deer and wild boar.

46

47